Rhymes & Reflections: Laughter, Love, and Life Lessons

Volume Two

Paperback Edition First Published in Great Britain 2024 by Dawn Wilkinson

ISBN: 9798324344177

Copyright © Dawn Wilkinson 2024

Dawn Wilkinson has asserted her rights under 'the Copyright Designs and Patents Act 1988' to be identified as the author of this work.

All rights reserved.

No part of this document may be reproduced or transmitted in any form or by any means, electronic, mechanical, photocopying, recording, or otherwise, without prior written permission of the Author.

Other books by Dawn Wilkinson

The eBay Series

An eBay life for me

Diary of an eBay seller

Where is my item?

*****

Self-Help and Manifestation

How to Manifest a life of PLEASURE

*****

Poetry

Rhymes and Reflections: Laughter, Love, and Life Lessons: Volume One

This book of poetry is dedicated to all the people who bring me joy – you know who you are!

I'm so blessed to have you in my life

In a world where trouble makers seem to be rife

You bring me calmness and peace

In this puzzle of my journey you're an important piece

To Lesley

love

Dawn xx

Foreword

I was delighted that Dawn asked me to write a foreword for her latest poetry book, in the first instance turning my thoughts to her latest ventures into the comedy circuit.

I then discerned that Dawn had chosen to share this as her most recent update so I began to reflect on how much she has achieved in the last couple of years. Not only has our friendship grown over this time but we have both been on a journey of creative development with our shared love of the written word and its many forms. We are blessed, we are in a unique position to support each other's writing.

Dawn has many special skills and attributes; her kindness and desire to help others is especially endearing. She is motivated to learn, develop and grow and she listens to the Universe. As if negotiating stepping stones across a river she has made choices that have guided her towards contemporary experiences and new life lessons. It seems that one thing has really led to another, opening up new possibilities and chances to re-invent herself. Dawn does not allow opportunities to slip away, she seizes them. Such opportunities exist for all of us yet we must be open minded and courageous to accept new challenges. Using individual skills to reach our full potential brings about a sense of true achievement.

I am often reminded of my school motto, *'Carpe Diem'*, an encouragement to focus on the present and appreciate the moment; it literally means *Seize the Day.* Make time for the things that are important to you and appreciate and enjoy the moments that lie ahead!

Angela Craddock

Introduction

Welcome to Volume Two – another delightful collection of 25 poems crafted just for you! Since the release of Volume One, the outpouring of positive feedback and encouragement has truly warmed my heart. It has been an eventful (and very busy) period indeed!

One of the highlights was embarking on a Comedy Course led by the talented comedians Cal Halbert and Alfie Joey. This exciting journey not only honed my comedic skills but also introduced me to a fantastic community of like-minded individuals. Together, we ventured into live shows, where our performances were met with resounding success.

In addition to honing my craft on stage, I have been actively participating in Open Mic nights, sharing my poetry with diverse audiences and embracing the vibrant atmosphere of artistic expression. Furthermore, I am thrilled to announce that I have secured two exciting events with North Tyneside Library, expanding the reach of my poetry to even more eager listeners.

And amidst all these adventures, I've been diligently working on launching my YouTube channel (Dawn Wilkinson), striving to create engaging content that resonates with viewers far and wide. Oh, and let's not forget, I've also managed to squeeze in a move to a new home – talk about a whirlwind of activity!

I am overjoyed to present this collection of poems to you. My aim is simple: to inspire, entertain, and bring a little more joy into your life through the power of poetry.

So sit back, relax, and immerse yourself in this poetic journey – I hope you enjoy it as much as I have enjoyed creating it for you.

Love Dawn xx

From 'Always Look on the Bright Side of Life'

If life seems jolly rotten (hoo-hoo)
There's something you've forgotten (hoo-hoo)
And that's to laugh and smile and dance and sing (hoo-hoo-hoo)
When you're feeling in the dumps (hoo-hoo)
Don't be silly, chumps (hoo-hoo)
Just purse your lips and whistle, that's the thing (hoo-hoo)
And

Always look on the bright side of life
(Come on)
Always look on the right side of life

Eric Idle (Monty Python)

Contents

Title	Page No.
The Game	17
New Year, New Plan	18
A Day In The Life Of Pixie	19
The Complaint	20
Inspired	22
Facebook	23
My Friend's Ex-Boyfriends	24
Excuses	26
Creep	27
Insomnia	28
Craig	30
Pigeons	32
The Not So Quiet Man	34
Earth Angel	35
The Medium	36
Dead Man Walking	38
The Good Old Days	40
Off Limits (Part One – Part Three)	42
Like A Lawsuit	46
Who Are You?	48
The Poached Egg	49
The Plumber	50
No More The Fool	52

Do Something	53
Bob and Jean	54
The story behind the poem	57
Inspirational Quotes	75
Other Titles Available (including some bonus poetry!)	79
About the Author	89

"I once went to one of those parties where everyone throws their car keys into the middle of the room. I don't know who got my moped, but I drove that Peugeot for years."

Victoria Wood

The Game

Is this a fair game when only you set the rules?

It seems you treat other players simply as fools

Who made you the rule maker?

Well, I'm finished with this sinister caper

You don't seem to consider your next move

You fail to realize it's yourself needing to improve

I'm sick of playing a game I can't win

On a positive note I've developed a thick skin

I'm done with this charade, I quit the game

I only wished you could have played fair, it's an unfortunate shame

Good luck with your next opponent, enjoy the moment

Because I know that it won't be too long for your day of atonement

New Year, New Plan

A new year, a new plan

I'm going to achieve all that I can

Spending time with people who bring me joy

Relationships that are toxic, I will destroy

Life's too short for sadness and dismay

Positivity and kindness are the spiritual way

There's no time for negativity and fear

This is going to be a fantastic year

So remember live each day to it's full potential

Making the most of this life experience is essential

A Day In The Life Of Pixie

I wake up and demand my food

I'll eat it all up, then reflect on my mood

If I'm still tired I'll go back to bed

To contemplate on my day ahead

After my nap I'll stroll around the house

Maybe scratch the carpet, then wait for the shouts

'Pixie stop that!' I clearly hear

I run away as the humans appear

My next job, continue with the wall-paper stripping

And that box over there, needs a damn good ripping

After all this work I need a rest

Another nap, I think, on their bed will be best!

The Complaint

'You should be ashamed of yourself' the message read

Oh, that's not the only thing the buyer said

'Selling faulty goods that simply don't work

You better resolve quickly, don't you dare shirk'

I can only apologize and ask for further details

'Please don't leave a negative, it can affect my sales'

'You sold me a trolley coin keyring

But when I tried to use it, it failed, that's the thing

I then went onto to try at three different stores

But worked at none of them, these faulty goods of yours

I demand my money back, and I might report you

For my humiliation I could even sue

People were laughing at me while I struggled

Under the pressure, I admit, I buckled'

'I'm so sorry to hear about this trouble with the product

An investigation into this matter I must conduct

I've sold hundreds of these, with no complaints what-so-ever

I'll get to the bottom of this, of that I promise to endeavour'

I test the trolley coins in stores aplenty

They all work perfectly, I tried at least twenty

I email the buyer and provide an update

I've refunded her payment so there's no need for hate

She replied and stated *'I owe you the money back*

I'm ever so sorry, I need to cut you some slack

On how to use one of these I clearly need training

You see, I didn't know the coin needed releasing from the keyring'

Inspired

Pink inspired me to get the party started

Whitney inspired me to find out what happened to the broken-hearted

Dolly Parton inspired me to persevere and try

Annie Lennox inspired me to always ask why

Cyndi Lauper inspired me to be strong

Abba inspired me to dance and sing-a-long

Debbie Harry inspired me to get that man

Shania inspired me to feel like a woman

Kate Bush inspired me to run up that hill

Enya inspired me to sit back and chill

Katy Perry inspired me to loudly roar

Bananarama inspired me to demand more

Kelly Clarkson inspired me to be forever grateful

Taylor Swift inspired me to never be hateful

Alanis inspired me to see the ironic

Madonna inspired me to simply be iconic

Facebook

Is Facebook healthy for you?

Do you think all entries through?

When someone disagrees with you does this lead to frustration?

For your opinions do you need validation?

Are you trying to impress others?

Are you desperately checking on ex-lovers?

Is it essential to provide hourly updates?

Can you really have satisfying debates?

Do you feel the need to like, comment and share every single post you see?

Do you need to point out every opinion with which you disagree?

Without Facebook could you survive?

Without Facebook would you feel deprived?

My Friend's Ex-Boyfriends

As I sat with a friend sharing a bottle of wine

We began to reminisce about men not so fine

Turns out she's had a fair few guys

Many more than I thought, an entertaining surprise

There was the Postman, Stu, who failed to deliver

The fisherman, John, preferred time on the river

That bastard binman, wouldn't take her out

The hunky stripper who shook it all about

Poet, Dean, left her for no rhyme or reason

The store Santa Claus stuck around for only one season

Dave, the Locksmith, would not open his heart

The Vicar, Dan, ran off with the local tart

The public speaker stubbornly refused to shut up

Bob, the Vet, only wanted to play with her pup

Don't mention the Doc, he gave her high blood pressure

The Driving Instructor, well, he just wanted to test her

The medium she couldn't trust, he was always seeing other people

That kinky Cake-Maker wanted to cover her in treacle

The Mechanic was only interested in her bodywork

The Footballer scored an own goal, the ultimate jerk

He screamed another name during passion, a painful blow

The flamboyant actor, well, he was just putting on a show

I console my friend and suggest we open another bottle

Together we'll make a list of the men we'd like to throttle

Excuses

Excuses, excuses, excuses; that's all you seem to make

You don't seem to realize this is your life at stake

Excuses won't bring you anything you desire

In fact, excuses will only put out the fire

Your life will never improve if you keep dodging action

Excuses will never bring you true satisfaction

The joy you feel when you achieve your dream

Is something you will never experience when the excuses stream

Excuses show that you have inner doubt

Trust in the Universe and you will never be without

The world can be your playground if you could only see

You've got to get out there to truly be free

Transformation can only occur and bring peace

When the self-doubt and excuses cease!

Creep

I've kept this to myself for so, so long

I feel it's now time to tell you, cos you're coming on strong

The truth of the matter is I think you're an arsehole

If you were the last man on earth I wouldn't touch you with a bargepole

You have an annoying laugh, and a deep dark stare

If you approach other women I'll be shouting beware!

Insomnia

I'm off to bed, tomorrow has plenty in store

A busy day ahead, lots to do, I can't take on more

The problem is as my head hits the pillow

Thoughts start entering my brain like a creeping willow

The sooner I get to sleep the sooner I can wake

I'm desperate for slumber make no mistake

I'm tossing and turning, it's quite concerning

I just can't get to sleep, and yes I've tried counting sheep!

It's midnight now, sleep must come soon

To the dream-world it seems I am immune

Should I get up and have a drink

Maybe a brandy would knock me out, I think

No, I can't do that, I need a clear head

Perhaps read a chapter from a book instead

It's now One o'clock, I put my book down

When am I going to get to sleep? I inwardly frown

Another hour goes by, I could sit and cry

Why can't I sleep, why oh why?

Its 3am I inwardly scream, staring at the clock

I'm mesmerized by the sound; tick tock

I give my pillow a squirt of lavender

My one wish tonight, to be an astral traveller

Please I need sleep, today I've got so much to do

With just a little shut eye I can still pull through

Come on you can do it, close your eyes and enter dream-state

It's no good, I desperately need help to sedate

Its 5am now, daylight I can see

But I can still get some hours, well maybe two or three

Time continues to pass by with still no kip

There's nowt I can do now, I need to get a grip

I start to make a list of things I can re-arrange

I'll be too tired now, my day I need to change

As I spread duties out over the coming days

I find myself entering a calm peaceful phase

With all this stress gone from my mind

I fall off to sleep and the dream-world I find

Craig

The day we met, had an immediate effect

Of the spiritual kind, a mutual respect

You were charismatic with a cheeky grin

Many happy times were about to begin

We enjoyed days out and trips to church

Your head in a book, always needing to research

You were an old soul it has to be said

With so much knowledge inside your young head

The day you left the physical world

Many questions inside my mind whirled

Why did you go and leave us behind?

Life can be cruel and so unkind

You promised to make contact in the note you left

But your physical absence has left many bereft

You sent me a feather, I claimed as mine

But it later flew away, to give another a sign

I'll never forget the day you passed broke my heart

For in my life you played a very special part

I was blessed to meet you, of that I know

With you on my spirit team, I continue to grow

Pigeons

<u>My perspective</u>

Why are you walking when you can bloody fly?

'Get off the road', I repeatedly cry

Can't you see these roads aren't suitable for you

Walking around without a bloody clue

Your mate over there is lying dead for all to see

If you don't move, your death I can clearly foresee

Pigeons

A Pigeon's Perception

I know I can fly but I want to walk

A leisurely stroll with a pal as we talk

I know you take issue with me walking on the road

But I don't see the problem truth be told

I know that you would love to fly around like me

Flying high in the skies, with beautiful scenery

My wings get tired soaring around all day

I love walking, it's the alternative way

For me to move about and enjoy my life

Though I'm really sorry to be causing you strife

I know you need to swerve that thing you drive

To not hit me and keep me alive

I appreciate that I really do

But let me live my life and you do what you do

The Not So Quiet Man

Here he comes, avoid his stare

I want to scream to others *'Please Beware'*

Once he sees you look his way

That's it you won't get rid of him for the rest of the day

He'll talk away about his plight

If you're not careful he'll go on all night

He has no consideration for what's going on in your life

He'll simply whinge on about his wife

Take my advice, if he comes near you

Run as fast as you can, even just to the loo

The not so quiet man really needs to hush down

It's time to grow up and stop playing the clown

You don't fool me, it's plain to see

Learning to respect others is the key

Earth Angel

You light up any room you enter

I'm pretty sure the angels sent ya

Into our lives you appeared from nowhere

Your zest for life you constantly share

You make our days special and exciting

You float around, charming and delighting

You are truly beautiful inside and out

Without you, life would be boring, we have no doubt

You make us laugh, you make life fun

From the moment we met you our hearts were won

The Medium

'Can I come to you, I've got a message from spirit'

I don't know what to expect, this is my first visit

The medium struts over and looks at me with delight

'You've recently seen spirit and you got such a fright'

'No, I don't recall anything, don't know what you're talking about'

'Well you will see spirit, of that I have no doubt

I have a man here, is dad in spirit?' The medium asks

'No he's very much alive, I seen him an hour ago in fact'

'Well, if it's not dad it's grandad, I only get family you see

Your grandad says just let things be'

'How do I know you have my grandad' I demand

I can see from my question things aren't going to plan

'Well, he's about the same height as me, maybe a bit taller

But then again, maybe a bit smaller'

I laugh and state **'Well, that doesn't make sense?**

All I want is some clear evidence

You're supposed to be a medium in touch with the dead

I don't think I'm being unreasonable' her face goes red

'He's not a great talker, that's the thing

Oh that's it he's gone, I'm not getting anything'

'Call yourself a medium, you had no message for me'

'Well yes I did, my dear, just let things be'

Dead Man Walking

This is the tale of a man guilty of murder

Was he born to kill or a product of nurture?

He killed his girlfriend, was it a crime of passion?

His victim, a true dedicated follower of fashion

New shoes, jackets, jewellery and bags

He was well pissed off as he sat in his rags

He thought to himself *'What a selfish bitch!'*

From love to hate he'd made the switch

A row erupted over her spending habit

He lost his temper and that was the end of Janet

The trial came soon, with a very strict judge

The death penalty issued, the judge wouldn't budge

The electric chair was the painful choice

'This is so unfair' the man voiced

Few states still used the chair, but this was Kentucky

And they still did, proving for him unlucky

Time ticked by as he sat in jail

He appealed and appealed but to no avail

One day he awoke, and as he stretched in his cell

He heard footsteps running and the sound of a bell

He was whisked off, head shaven and fitted with a cap

Oh, on that fateful day he wished he hadn't snapped

He suddenly realised this was his execution date

The priest entered the room with a brief update

'Any last requests – Please state your demands'

'Yes' said the man *'Can you hold my hand?'*

The Good Old Days

I remember the good old days, when the air was clean and the sex was dirty

Men could be men, and ever so flirty

You could go out and be on your own

You never went anywhere carrying a phone

There was no such thing as a download

You simply went to Woolworths' down the road

You could hire a VHS from the rental store

Taking it back was the only chore

You taped the charts off the radio onto cassette

Missing the DJ's voice was the time to sweat

We sometimes got post twice a day

Cash was king, it was the preferred way to pay

With limited choice of TV channels

And there was no such thing as LCD panels

We had pop icons with classic music

And remember that puzzle so great, the must have Rubik

Of course, we don't like to remember the yesteryear fashion

And we can no longer mention some National Treasures with compassion

But I still loved the good old days

It was completely different to this present phase!

Off Limits (Part One)

It all started so innocent, but things didn't go to plan

So, let's begin I'll tell my story the best I can

'Let's watch a film tonight', my boyfriend declared

'What about a horror? We'll hold each other if we get scared'

The movie starts and his hand creeps closer

I unzip his jeans for full exposure

Our hands rip at each others clothes

We know longer care how the film goes

We writhe around in great delight

I'm not a tart, but I'm putting up no fight

'Take me' I scream **'Right Now, Right Here!'**

We clear the space, with absolutely no fear

We hear a noise and are disrupted

We quickly get up and clothes are adjusted

It seems our behaviour has left many mentally scarred

That is how from the *cinema* we were barred

Off Limits (Part Two)

My boyfriend had an idea so unique

I'll admit when he shared it, I let out a shriek

He wants to re-enact sex scenes from the silver screen

I'm instantly excited and clearly keen

Things went well for quite a while

We took it seriously and always went the extra mile

9 ½ weeks kept us very busy indeed

This was racy as hell we both agreed

Many films were ticked off our list

We watched some again in case there was something we missed

Then we discovered a movie called **'Dark Desire'**

I'm burning up, am I on fire?

There's a shower scene we were desperate to act out

'We haven't got a shower' I sadly pout

My boyfriend said **'Don't worry, I've got a plan'**

I also add, *'Running water I need to ban*

I'm scared I'll fall and slip,

I could easily break a hip'

He agreed, so I left him in charge

Anyway that's how from *B and Q* we were barred

Off Limits (Part Three)

My man had that look in his eye as he looked my way

He asked *'Do you really want to make my day'*

'Hell yes, what can I do? Shall I take you to Rome?'

'No' he replied *'I want to make love in every room in the home'*

'Not a problem' I smile, **'We will start in the lounge'**

It wasn't long till that special spot he found

Next on the list was the Office Space

The desk took a bashing, it'll need to be replaced

On the Kitchen counter he threw me upon

He's bloody hot stuff, a Geordie Don Juan

The Dining table was unusually tricky

Something must have spilt cos it was rather sticky

The boring bedroom was next on the list

Till someone screamed *'Are you taking the piss?*

We were shocked to see an angry security guard

And that's how from *Ikea* we were barred

Like a Lawsuit

Madonna's in trouble and I think it's so unfair

All the criticism she's facing I really can't bear

Poor Madge is being sued for starting her concerts late

There might be good reasons – she doesn't deserve hate

Perhaps the night before she had a dodgy vindaloo

The reason for her lateness – she couldn't get off the loo

Or perhaps her younger lover had a massive erection

It's understandable she'd need to give it closer inspection

Perhaps she was practising her masturbation scene

She got carried away and added more to the routine

Where the hell have you been if you don't know her reputation?

She's probably arrived on stage late in every nation

Did you ever consider that she is getting old?

The pains she could be suffering are maybe untold

What if she had an accident and gone arse over tits?

Just like she did years ago during her set at the Brits

Let's cut her some slack and respect her like a pro

It goes without saying she puts on a hell of a show

Is this lawsuit just two fans trying their luck?

Whatever the case, I doubt Madonna gives a flying F***!

Who Are You?

I've met all types of people during this journey

From my plans and dreams not one can deter me

I've encountered the cheeky, sarcastic, and plain rude

From humble to obnoxious, and slightly crude

But I endeavour to learn from all of these folk

Knowing there's always a small few aiming to provoke

The lesson I've learned over the years

Is never give in to irrational fears

It's clear you have issues with your own self-esteem

That's why you seem unable to work as a team

I've met many people in this life

There's always someone plotting to twist in the knife

I'm diligent, cautious, and extremely wise

To your hostility I will not rise

Are you a sociopath or narcissistic?

Or are you simply an arrogant egotistic?

Who are you? I don't really care

Because with you, my time and energy I'm not willing to share

The Poached Egg

The dream of the perfect poached egg I pursue

But I can only try my best, what else can I do?

No matter how hard I've tried

I can only manage scrambled or fried

I take inspiration from the chefs of the nation

But this only leads to more frustration

I've tried vinegar in and vinegar out

My repeated failures make me want to scream and shout

My attempts always end up in the bin

It seems that I simply can't win

I followed the recipe book procedure

I whisked so hard, I nearly brought on a seizure

It's got to the point I can't look at an egg

'Can someone please help?' I constantly beg

The one thing I can finally boast

I make cracking beans on toast!

The Plumber

My friend had an idea so bright

She needed a plumber but money was tight

Choosing to give Mybuilder a miss

She joined a dating site, she couldn't resist

Her plan was quite simple she stated

She entered her details, sat back and waited

Seeking a man who was handy and skilled

Many DIY jobs were needing fulfilled

Her cunning ploy was to attract a fit plumber

She needed her pipes cleaned ideally before summer

A young man called Dennis got in touch

He said he liked her profile picture very much

They arranged a date which went extremely well

He was eager to come back to hers of that she could tell

Once she had him in her grips

Dragged him to the bathroom to assess her drips

While he got busy with the repairs

She sauntered on back down the stairs

'I've hit the jackpot' she thought, preparing a drink

Sitting back relaxing, while he fixed the sink

Later that night, several bottles of wine they shared

And then he cleaned her pipes she happily declared!

No More The Fool

No more the fool who'll wait for you

To see the error of your ways and stop being cruel

No more the fool who will put up with disrespect

With no consideration for cause and affect

No more the fool who will play your game

It's always someone else's fault you repeatedly proclaim

No more the fool who doesn't speak up

When you constantly moan about your half empty cup

No more the fool who cares for you

Your character and purpose is under review

Do Something

Wake every morning with eagerness and zest

Go out there and give it your best

Look for opportunities for you to excel

Laziness you must always repel

Give everything you do one hundred percent

Never envy others, hate or resent

You will only know what you can achieve

When you try, and try again, have faith and believe

Bob and Jean

Bob sat and thought how he could spice up his life

He wanted exciting sex with his long-suffering wife

He'd watched many documentaries to give him some insight

About what others did late at night

He plucked up the courage to start the conversation

He told her *'I'm bored and I need your participation*

Would you consider BDSM? He asked

'Well, I prefer 'Home Bargains' she answered at last

'No, No, that's not what I mean, I want adventure in the bedroom

How about we re-decorate and make it a sex room?'

'What! All that work when you only ever lasted five minutes

You're living in a dream-world, you need to know your limits!'

'I'm frustrated!' he screamed *'I want exhilaration'*

'Oh behave yourself, your health is in major deterioration'

'How about dogging?' he finally cried

'Oh no, I could never have another dog since Bruno died!'

'No, no, no, you're not grasping this

I'm talking about sex – please don't resist'

'That's it, I'm not listening to this any more

One more word, and I''ll show you the door

You're a walking war zone, you ache in every bone

Carry on like this and you'll be on your own

You're not a young man any more

Time's limited to find new things to explore

Let's sit for awhile in each others arms

Remember when we met I fell for your charms'

They cuddled up together as they sat and smiled

'I love you so much' he stated with tears in his eyes

'You were wild and free, knowing how to tantalize

I wouldn't change a thing after all these years

What we have together is all I need it appears'

'Oh, you're so cute and how I adore you still

Now let's get to the bedroom for an afternoon thrill!'

The Story Behind The Poem

The Game

In our journey through life, we often encounter individuals who revel in playing intricate mind games. This poem draws its inspiration from one such person who seems to derive pleasure from these manipulative tactics. Yet, through experience, I've uncovered a valuable trick: simply refuse to engage in their games altogether.

Why waste time and energy on a futile endeavour? What satisfaction is there in participating in a game rigged against you from the start? It is when you realize that these individuals are consumed by the need for control. They also often lack contentment in their own lives. Their penchant for mind games stems from a deep-seated desire to exert dominance over others.

But we hold the power to break free from their web of manipulation. We possess the ability to firmly say no, to set boundaries, and to safeguard our peace of mind. The essence of this poem is a reminder: Don't squander your precious energy on something inherently fruitless. Refuse to fuel their behaviour with attention, for it only perpetuates their cycle of control and dissatisfaction. Instead, redirect your focus towards endeavours that nourish your soul and lead to genuine fulfilment.

New Year, New Plan

I penned this poem on New years Day 2024. For many, 1st January symbolizes a clean slate, a chance to shed old habits and embrace transformative change. It marks a moment of introspection, a time to assess one's journey thus far and chart a course towards personal growth and improvement.

At the heart of this poem lies a profound truth: the power of positivity to manifest greatness.

> *"The object of a new year is not that we should have a new year, but rather that we should have a new soul."*
>
> **Gilbert K. Chesterton**

A Day in the Life of Pixie

This poem is about our gorgeous tabby cat, Pixie. I love cats, and it amazes me how their personalities come through. Pixie is a character! She loves her food, her sleep, and her daddy, in that order. I get some attention when she feels like it. This poem is a fun look at daily life for Pixie.

The Complaint

As an eBay seller for over 17 years, I have received various complaints over the years. Believe it or not, I hadn't received a great number of complaints until the postal strikes of 2022. I was inundated with complaints of 'Item not received' nature due to the Royal Mail strikes. I compiled these complaints into a book called 'Where is my item?' available on Amazon now (shameless plug).

In my first book 'An eBay Life for me' (Available on Amazon) I shared the complaint about a faulty trolley keyring. This complaint inspired this poem and basically follows the conversation I had with a disgruntled buyer. This lady purchased a trolley coin keyring which I promptly dispatched. Not long after I received a message stating that I should be ashamed of myself for selling faulty goods. I immediately sprang into action and tested the trolley coins at various super-markets. I updated her with my findings. I then received a message offering an apology. The buyer had not known they needed to release the coin from the keyring in order to use it. Yes, unbelievable but true!

Inspired

Anyone who knows me is aware of my love for music. Madonna being my ultimate favourite. However, I have been inspired by so many artists throughout my life. You will notice all the artists mentioned in this poem are women (except the reference to Abba). I will be writing another poem in the future featuring male artists.

Never under-estimate the power of music to uplift your soul. Whenever you feel down stick some music on and forget your troubles. I encourage you to think about the songs you love and create your own playlist to help uplift in times of low moods.

Facebook

I make no secret of the fact I do not like Facebook. Although I am on Facebook I rarely check it and never enter any personal information. I don't believe in updating people of my every move (or meal!), that said I am aware there may be benefits to using Facebook. It's just not for me!

So many people live their lives trying to impress others. Get out there, live your life and stop worrying about getting 'likes' and 'comments'.

"Facebook should really have a "no one cares about" option too."

Unknown

My Friend's Ex-Boyfriends

The Ex-boyfriends poem featured in Rhymes and Reflections Volume One has been a huge hit with people. At Open-Mic nights I was frequently asked to perform the Ex-Boyfriends poem. This inspired me to write a follow up. I thought it would be interesting to write about a friend's ex-boyfriends.

It's basically a list of one-liners I thought of which I feel works well in poetry form.

Excuses

One thing that really disappoints me in life is how some people so easily give up on a better life and constantly seem to make excuses. So many people never unleash their full potential due to self-doubt. When self-doubt creeps in that's when the excuses start. If you really want something you will not give up at the first hurdle. You will endeavour to persevere and find a way around the hurdle. Stop making excuses and start living the life you have prevented yourself from experiencing.

"He that is good for making excuses is seldom good for anything else."

Benjamin Franklin

Creep

I'm not going to say much about this poem, I'll let it speak for itself.

Insomnia

"Sometimes you lie in bed at night and you don't have a single thing to worry about. That always worries me!"
Charlie Brown

This poem was inspired by, Surprise,Surprise, a night of tossing and turning. That feeling when you check the clock as every hour passes and you console yourself with; well you can still get a few hours.

"Nothing cures insomnia faster than the realization it's time to get up."
Unknown

Craig

This poem is about my good friend Craig. Sadly, Craig took his own life in July 2020. I originally met Craig at a Spiritualist Church and as he stood to deliver a message during an Open Circle, my mother and I instantly fell in love with his gentle charm. We became firm friends. We enjoyed many trips to

Churches around the North East and completed work shops together. We'd often meet up for meals and shopping trips.

I will never forget watching Craig's first Demonstration of Mediumship Service. He looked so smart in his suit. My mother and I sat in the front row sending positive vibes his way. We still talk about that night and the feeling of immense pride we felt for him.

A gentle kind-hearted and wisely soul. Craig promised he would be in touch from the other side and I am so pleased I can confirm he has. I know he is now on my spiritual team helping to guide me.

Pigeons

I wrote this poem after observing pigeons walking on the road. I was frustrated and asked why they would walk on the road when they can fly. Then I thought about reasons why the pigeons might prefer walking instead of flying. It's a little fun look at how pigeons behave.

The Not So Quiet Man

This poem is inspired by a chatterbox in a cafe I used to frequent. The man who inspired this poem has a reputation for starting conversations with people and then refusing to leave their table. Even when told to politely leave he still ignores requests and continues to dominate conversations.

"It's very important in life to know when to shut up. You should not be afraid of silence."

Alex Trebek

Earth Angel

I penned this poem with a lovely friend in mind. Of course, I'm blessed to have so many lovely people in my life, this poem can apply to those as well.

Even when people move on and aren't in your life any more, never forget the positive memories you have of them. Always know you met them for a reason. Some people are meant to be on this journey the whole way through and others are here to share a short period with you. People are sent into our lives for many different reasons. Some people help you and provide opportunities to expand your experiences and some people are simply sent to teach you lessons.

"I believe friends are quiet angels who lift us to our feet when our wings have trouble remembering how to fly."

Unknown

The Medium

Over the years I have witnessed thousands of demonstrations of Mediumship. Unfortunately, there are some people claiming to be mediums who are quite simply deluded or not striving to give an evidential message. This poem is a humorous look at someone claiming to be a medium giving a message with no evidence to prove who the spirit person is.

A medium who I do admire is Gordon Higginson. Gordon, in my opinion, provided clear evidence from the spirit world.

I reproduce the following article available from *Psychic News, 17th October 1953*

BROTHER AND SISTER DIED WITHIN A MONTH – COME BACK TOGETHER

A brother and sister who died within a month of each other returned together to greet their mother during Gordon Higginson's demonstration of clairaudience at the Luton National Spiritualist Church's meeting on Saturday of last week. Gordon Higginson was sharing the platform at this meeting, which was held in the Beech Hill School, with Doris Greenwell.

Typical of Higginson's style was the fact that the message involved several people. To a man and woman sitting at the side of the hall Higginson spoke of the name Graysley. Neither of them could understand this, but when Gordon referred to a Joyce, the woman said: "Oh, yes; I can place it now. The name is Gazeley."

"Joyce is a youngish person who passed to spirit," said the medium, and, receiving recognition, added, "She is speaking of Christopher." "Yes," said the woman." They lived..." Gordon paused as he listened clairaudiently for the address, "they lived at Number 10..." "Yes." "...Number 10 Ickley Close," concluded Higginson, a statement which brought confirmation.

At this stage Gordon remarked that Joyce had met a Lilian Jean in spirit who was also manifesting. Neither of the two recipients could place Lilian Jean, and the clairaudient added: "She says, 'My mother is here.'"

At that Mrs. F. Elkerton, who is associated with the church, and lives at 492 Dunstable Road, Luton, called out that it probably referred to her, as she had a daughter in spirit named Jean Lilian.

RELATED

That it was indeed intended for Mrs. Elkerton, who is related to the two previous recipients, was proved by the following conversation. Said Higginson: "She says that her brother is with her." There was a pause, and he gave the name, "Frank Ernest." "That's right," said Mrs. Elkerton.

"There was a tragic double passing," said the medium. "They passed within a little time of each other. They were about the same ages." As the recipient confirmed these dramatic facts,

Gordon said: "They have come with Joyce, who sends her love to Eric."

After the meeting Mrs. Elkerton explained to our reporter the relationship of these names. Eric, she said, was Joyce's husband who was still on earth. Christopher was her little boy, and Joyce was her daughter-in-law. As far as she knew, there was no way in which Gordon could have known these facts, she told Psychic News.

There was one short, but very evidential message, which Higginson delivered to a man at the back of the hall. He mentioned a name like Acheson, which brought a response, and said that the communicator had passed on in a Japanese Prisoner of War camp after his ship – it sounded like S.S. Kirkdale – had gone down. This was readily acknowledged by the recipient, who also understood references to a baker named Hyde and Dallow Road.

Several messages of similar vein were transmitted by Gordon Higginson in a three-quarter-hour demonstration.

Dead Man Walking

This poem was actually inspired by a joke.

A man on death row facing the electric chair on his execution day was asked by the priest 'Have you any final wishes?'

The man replied 'Yes, can you hold my hand?'

The tale of a crime of passion was inspired by my interest in True Crime stories.

The Good Old Days

One of my friends, Liverpool Dawn, stated one day, *'I remember the good old days, when the air was clean and the sex was dirty'.* This statement inspired this poem. A look back at yesteryear. The things we had then and alas no more.

I hope you liked this poem as it's a trip down memory lane. I remember going to Woolworths' to buy the latest pop song I had heard on the radio. Of course, I didn't have the money to buy all the songs (I loved) in the charts. I would wait patiently for the Sunday charts on the radio and tape the hits I wanted. I'll admit I would call the DJ names when he interrupted the beginning or ending of a song.

Off Limits (Part One to Three)

This trio of poems was inspired during a comedy course I completed in January and February 2024. It was a seven week course which enabled us to write our own stand-up comedy set. I must stress this is all fiction (well most of it!) I am not barred from anywhere for sexual exploits. Having said that it might be a good thing for me to be barred from Ikea, Gary says we would save a fortune!

I also confess I have not seen the film 'Dark Desire' I simply googled 'Sexiest sex scene in a shower.' I must watch it though!

Like A Lawsuit

Again, this poem was penned as part of my comedy course. One week our homework was to write a sketch based on a current news story. As a Madonna fan, I found the news that she was going to be sued for coming on stage late during her 'Celebration' tour amusing. I have seen Madonna live numerous times and during my experiences the shows never started on time. As a Madonna fan I wanted to defend her. This poem is a little tongue-in-cheek at possible excuses for Madonna's lateness.

I also produced this joke statement from Madonna's point of view (incorporating some Madonna song titles):

I'm being accused of being a **Bad girl.** It's no **Secret, I'm a sinner** with a **Rebel Heart** . I've never been an **Angel Pretender.** I do feel this libel case is unfair.

My patience has been pushed to the **Borderline** and I've told my father, **Papa don't preach.** W**hy's it so hard** to cut me some slack? **You must love me**. I've always kept people **Waiting.**

Don't tell me what time I need to get my ass on stage. Yo **Bitch, I'm Madonna** you need to **Cherish** me. It may seem like I'm an **Unapologetic Bitch** because that's what I am. I feel you ungrateful bastards are **Causing a commotion,** which has got me **Burning up** I've got a bloody **Fever** now. You clearly don't care about my health, I nearly died last year you know. But you just **Can't stop** picking fault with me. **Everybody** else seems happy with the show, it's a true **Celebration** of my career in **Music.**

What do you want from me? Do you want me to **Take a bow**'? Do you want me to say **Bye bye baby,** Cos that's not going to happen. **Like it or not** I don't need your **Intervention,** I'm not **Sorry**. You know I'll turn up **Sooner or Later** well okay never sooner!

I want you to show me some respect. However, **Like a virgin** I will learn from this experience cos you've well and truly tried to screw me over. Even if you gave me **One more chance** I'd still arrive late **Over and over**. I won't even **Promise to try, You'll see**. I'm so angry you should thank your **Lucky star**s I haven't got a **Revolver.**

So my shows **Used to be your playground**, but I don't want these suing **Vulgar** bastards at my shows in the **Future**, there will be no **Get together** offer from me. They'll have to sit at home and **Turn up the radio.** Yes I know I'm a **Girl Gone Wild.**

I need a bloody **Holiday!**

Who Are You?

Have you ever had that experience when you meet someone for the first time and pick up negative vibes? Sometimes you just can't decide if this person likes you. I don't waste energy trying to make people like me. If you don't like me I'm not going to worry about it, and I'm certainly not going to change in order to win your approval.

On a positive note, I have learned recently that some people who come across as rude or unfriendly often have other issues going on in their lives. I have learned not to take things personally. Be friendly, where possible, as you will be surprised how this can break barriers down. Always surround yourself with positive minded people and avoid negativity wherever possible.

If you don't like me, remember it's mind over matter.
I don't mind, and you don't matter.

Dr. Seuss

The Poached Egg

While out for a meal one day a friend confided that she had never been able to make poached eggs. A conversation started with everyone chipping in tips and hints on how to achieve the perfect poached egg. She frustratingly replied to every comment with *'I've tried that!'*

This conversation inspired the poem about the frustration felt with every failed attempt!

The Plumber

One day at a warm welcome meeting at a local church I engaged in conversation with a lovely man called Dennis. He was a retired plumber. He shared stories with me about his working life and also how sometimes housewives would proposition the workmen. I devised the poem inspired by Dennis (but I stress not about him!)

I wondered if any ladies advertise on dating sites not only looking for love but a handy man with a drill or a plumber.

No More The Fool

This poem is inspired by reaching the end of the line with someone in your life. The realization point when you now know the person you have tolerated and given ample opportunities to are simply not going to change their ways.

You get what you tolerate

This poem was inspired by the classic song 'No More The Fool' by Elkie Brooks:

> *Just why I stayed around*
> *When all I found was heartache*
> *I believed your every word*
> *Didn't know the hurt and pain that you'd make*
> *But why did it take so long*
> *At last now I've seen the light*
> *I've found the heart to say*
>
> *No more the fool who waits around*
> *Waiting for you to bring me down*

This poem is about stating enough is enough. It's about setting boundaries and demanding more for yourself.

"Lack of boundaries invites lack of respect."

Anonymous

Do Something

Inspired by Dave Fishwick. Dave is a businessman who wanted to start his own high street bank. When the banks refused loans to struggling businesses, Dave stepped in and set his own bank up. However, he has faced much opposition from the banking industry. There is a film called '**Bank of Dave'** about his story. He is a truly inspirational man. His motto is 'Do something, cos it's always better than doing nothing'. Hence, the inspiration for this poem.

Bob and Jean

This is possibly my favourite poem. One of my favourite comedy sketches is the classic Victoria Wood's *Let's Do it* song. I wanted to write a poem reflecting how an older couple might view the importance of sex. With so many shows on television now about dating and sex I wondered how an elderly couple might be influenced. As we can see from the poem, Bob was clearly intrigued by this content and wanted to explore. While, Jean is happy with a cuddle from Bob and wants an easy life, ever cautious of Bob's failing health. I added the two lines at the end of the poem after many people indicated (during open mic nights) they would like a smuttier ending.

I hope you have enjoyed Volume Two as much as I have enjoyed writing these poems.

Til next time, Keep smiling!   *Love Dawn xx*

Inspirational Quotes

The aim of my poetry is in inspire, and entertain. Sometimes, one quote can change your perception about life. These next few pages include some favourite quotes I have stumbled across during my pursuit to understand this life!

Life is like the stock market. Some days you're up. Some days you're down. And some days you feel like something the bull left behind.

Paula Wall

Be miserable. Or motivate yourself. Whatever has to be done, it's always your choice.

Wayne Dyer

People say money is not the key to happiness, but I have always figured if you have enough money, you can have a key made.

Joan Rivers

Do not take life too seriously. You will never get out of it alive.

Elbert Hubbard

You only live once, but if you do it right, once is enough.

Mae West

I love mankind... it's people I can't stand!!

Charles M. Schulz

Would I rather be feared or loved? Easy. Both. I want people to be afraid of how much they love me.

Michael Scott, *The Office*

I have a lot of growing up to do. I realized that the other day inside my fort.

Zach Galifianakis

Lots of people want to ride with you in the limo, but what you want is someone who will take the bus with you when the limo breaks down.

Oprah Winfrey

I drink to make other people more interesting.
Ernest Hemingway

Wine is constant proof that God loves us and loves to see us happy.
Benjamin Franklin

The secret of staying young is to live honestly, eat slowly, and lie about your age.
Lucille Ball

Be wise, because the world needs wisdom. If you cannot be wise, pretend to be someone who is wise, and then just behave like they would.
Neil Gaiman

People who think they know everything are a great annoyance to those of us who do.
Isaac Asimov

One Day or Day One – It's Your Decision.

Other Titles available by Dawn Wilkinson

(Including some bonus poetry!)

An eBay life for me

An eBay life for me
Flutterbuys123
Always bargains there will be
Yes, it's an eBay life for me

Are you stuck in miserable employment and want to change career?
Make money selling online and enjoy the freedom and flexibility of being your own boss. 'An eBay Life for me' is the perfect starter guide to help you delve into the world of online selling. This book includes practical advice on how to source stock, pack items to ensure safe delivery, useful tips to help you buy items that will return good profit.

Dawn Wilkinson has been an online seller for over 14 years and has acquired over 96,000 positive feedback.
She has an excellent reputation online.

"Whether you would like to make extra money from selling online by decluttering your own belongings or simply wish to sell online and be your own boss. This book will provide the knowledge you need in order to do so.

This is a simple, concise book, containing step by step instructions, tips and advice on how to sell online successfully.

Dawn Wilkinson is a vastly experienced and successful 'eBay™ entrepreneur' with many years of selling experience on an online platform. And in this excellent, inspirational book she shares many amusing stories and sound advice to inspire you.

Dawn has been a full-time eBay™ seller since 2007 with an over 96,000 positive feedback score.

Within these pages you will find much practical information to help you start your own online business.

Including: This book will definitely be your first step on the road to becoming a highly successful part or full-time eBay™ seller!"
John Hamer, author.

Chapters include information on:

- **Researching and sourcing stock**
- **Step by step guide on how best to list an item to attract more potential buyers**
- **Handy tips to ensure you pack your items correctly to avoid damaged items in the post**
- **How to deal with Customer queries and complaints**
- **Useful tips to help you avoid making mistakes that cost you money**

- **Applying this useful advice to sell on other online sales websites. It also includes tips on how to sell successfully at car boot sales.**
- **Plus more!**

Recent reviews include:

Nic Hills -"Its a really good read." *(check out YouTube video : 'We are in a book' Nic Hills)*
(Check out Nic and Andrea Hills You Tube Channel for some very informative videos to help your online business)

Dawn Wilkinson's mam -"I've read it. It's actually very good!"

Amazon Customer -"This book is amazing in that it's easy to follow"

Amazon Customer - "What a fabulous book for would be Ebay sellers. Full of practical help from beginning to end interspersed with humour as the author relates charming little stories. Totally refreshing, a great read!"

Amazon Customer - "Must have for everyone! Some great tips to help anyone wishing to sell online along with entertaining tales!"

Diary of an eBay seller

Are you an eBay seller looking for some comic relief? Look no further than Dawn Wilkinson's hilarious diary of an eBay seller! Written by a seasoned eBay seller, this diary chronicles the ups and downs of selling online. Here are just a few reasons why you'll love this book:

- **Funny mishaps**
- **Inspiring successes**: This diary includes stories of successful sales and entrepreneurial triumphs. You'll be inspired by Dawn's stories.
- **Practical tips:** Along the way, this book offers practical tips and advice for eBay sellers. You'll learn how to avoid common mistakes, streamline your operations, and maximize your profits. Also included for Dawn's own entertainment tips for good movies to watch!
- **Relatable experiences**: As an eBay seller, you've likely experienced some of the same challenges and triumphs as our author. You'll feel a sense of camaraderie and community as you read about the author's experiences.
- **Entertaining read**: Above all, this diary is just plain fun to read. It's the perfect escape from the stress of running an eBay business, and will leave you feeling uplifted and inspired.

Whether you're a new seller or a seasoned pro, Dawn Wilkinson's 'Diary of an eBay seller' is a must-read. Order now and get ready to laugh, learn, and be inspired by the hilarious mishaps and inspiring successes of the eBay selling world.

Following the success of Dawn's first book, *'An eBay life for me - Tips and Advice on How to Sell,'* she now shares with us her diary-style sequel. You are invited to take a day out of life to read this amusing reflection of her unusual interactions and encounters.
Walk with her through the seasons and experience the highs and occasional lows of running her Flutterbuys123 business.

As a top rated seller Dawn reflects on how she can provide exceptional customer service whilst striving to be a better version of herself. She derives motivation from inspirational quotes scattered through the pages, proving to us that a positive attitude can make things happen.

Whether you plan to start your own business or simply aim to list some ad hoc items, you will benefit from the tips and pitfalls derived from Dawn's vast experience.
Discover also how to become a better eBay buyer!

Learn how to:
- Take advantage of sunny days and make money on rainy days
- Holiday away from negativity and embrace positivity
- Source your stock and make pleasing profit
- Create opportunities to harness personal success.

Life doesn't always run smoothly though we all have the ability to let love shine and make things better. Take a page out of Dawn's book and who knows where this journey of discovery may lead you - Angela Craddock, author.

Where is my item?

A collection of messages received during Royal Mail strike period of 2022 and how it affected my business and others, On a positive note looking at protecting your income in the future.

A funny look at the most difficult time for an online trader: Postal strikes! A collection of messages showing the diversity of characters. One of the funniest comments I received: The delay is nothing to do with the postal strikes????

Where is My Item?

'Where is my item?' Oh how I hate this question
As an eBay seller it causes much tension
You see, I post all my items as quickly as I can
But after that it's in the hands of the Royal Mail Postman

'Where is my item? It has not arrived
I don't think you posted it!' a buyer derived
It has been posted, your patience I appreciate
I can only apologize if your parcel is late

'Where is my item? I need it now'
I pray for its arrival as I wipe my brow
I always reply *'I'm so sorry for the delay'*
All these complaints are making me go grey!

How to Manifest a Life of PLEASURE

Advice and Exercises to help you achieve a happy life Unlock the secrets to living a happier, more fulfilling life with this transformative guidebook. "How to Manifest a Life of PLEASURE" is a comprehensive set of principles and exercises designed to help you embrace joy, abundance, and satisfaction in every aspect of your life.

Say goodbye to stress and dissatisfaction, and start living a life filled with pleasure and happiness!

Don't wait any longer to start living a life filled with pleasure and happiness. Grab your copy of "How to Manifest a Life of PLEASURE" today and embark on a transformative journey towards a happier, more satisfying existence. Your future self will thank you!

Rhymes & Reflections: Laughter, Love, and Life Lessons Volume One

Dive into a world where laughter dances hand in hand with sentimentality, and inspiration blooms from the essence of everyday moments. "Rhymes & Reflections" is not just a poetry collection; it's an invitation to embrace the myriad shades of life through verse.

Unwind with poems that tickle your funny bone, crafted with wit and charm to bring a smile to your face.

Delve into heartfelt pieces that navigate the complexities of human emotions, celebrating love, loss, and the beauty of resilience.

Find solace and motivation within verses that resonate with your soul, offering wisdom and insight into life's unpredictable journey.

About the Author

Dawn Wilkinson lives in Newcastle Upon Tyne with her partner, Gary, and their two fur-babies, Pixie and Dexter. Dawn believes a positive outlook on life is beneficial to our physical and mental well-being.

If you want like to connect with Dawn she is available on the following platforms:

Twitter	@Flutterbuys123
YouTube	Dawn Wilkinson @eBayflutterbuys123
Facebook	Dawn Flutterbuys
eBay	Flutterbuys123
Etsy	Flutterbuys123

Dawn's books are available on Amazon.

Flutterbuys Designs Notebooks are also available on Amazon.

You can also contact Dawn direct: www.dawnwilkinson.co.uk

"I told the doctor I broke my leg in two places. He told me to quit going to those places."

Henny Youngman

Printed in Poland
by Amazon Fulfillment
Poland Sp. z o.o., Wrocław